Embroidery Machine Essentials
Appliqué Techniques

Mary Mulari

©2004 Mary Mulari
Published by

kp krause publications
An imprint of F+W Publications, Inc.

700 East State Street • Iola, WI 54990-0001
715-445-2214 • 888-457-2873
www.krause.com

Our toll-free number to place an order or to obtain a free catalog is 800-258-0929

ISBN 0-87349-847-X

Edited by Jeanine Twigg
Designed by Marilyn McGrane

Printed in the United States of America

Table of Contents

Foreword 4

Introduction 4

Chapter 1 - Appliqué Essentials 5

Design Choices 6
   Design Segments 7
   Practice Stitch Samples 8
   Copyright 8
Embroidery Supplies 9
   Stabilizers 9
      Tear-away 9
      Cut-away 9
      Water-soluble 9
   Appliqué Adhesives 10
   Temporary Spray Adhesive 10
   Fusible Adhesive 10
   Thread 10
   Needles 11
   Scissors 11
   Interfacing 11

Chapter 2 - Traditional Appliqué Techniques 12

About Appliqué 13
Fabric Choices 14
Hooping 15
Stitch & Trim Appliqué 16
Template Appliqué 17
Reverse Appliqué 19

Chapter 3 - Creative Appliqué Techniques 20

Allover Stitch Appliqué 21
Raw-Edge Appliqué 23
Frayed-Edge Appliqué 24
Liberated Appliqué 25
   Water-soluble Base 25
   Anne's Pins 25
   Sheer Fabric Base 26
Padded Appliqué 26
Dimensional Appliqué 27
Sheer & Lace Appliqué 28
Textured Appliqué 29
Echo Appliqué 30
Fabricless Appliqué 30
Patchwork Appliqué 31

Chapter 4 - Appliqué Accents 32

Beads, Bangles & Buttons 33
Movable Appliqué 35
   Appliqués as Luggage Tags 34
Patches and Pockets 36
Frames for Appliqué 37
Combining Designs 37

Chapter 5 - Gallery of Project Ideas 38

Resources 43

Appendix - Design Details 44

Recommended Reading 48

CD-ROM Instructions 48

Foreword

Appliqué is my favorite embroidery technique. It's fast, easy, and fun to mix fabric with embroidery stitches. As an added bonus, appliqué saves time embroidering, allowing more time for creating fun projects! When planning the next book in the *Embroidery Machine Essentials, Companion Project Series*, I instantly thought of working with appliqué expert, Mary Mulari, to produce a book dedicated to creative appliqué techniques.

Welcome to Mary's world of appliqué! She has created a series of unique designs and techniques that go beyond traditional satin stitches. You're in for a real treat!

Jeanine

Introduction

I have been drawing and sewing appliqué designs since 1982. My first try at satin stitching produced wavy and irregular self-guided shapes, with gaps and an obvious lack of stitch control. I experimented and discovered the importance of fusible products, stabilizers, and sewing machine settings. Practice is what makes appliqué stitching on the sewing machine perfect, or at least much more attractive! It was satisfying to watch my stitching improve as I continued experimenting.

Then came the embroidery machine with its ability to produce perfect stitches. I was excited about appliqués being embroidered in a fraction of the time it would take on a sewing machine. I coined the term "automatic appliqué" to distinguish appliqué on an embroidery machine from the self-guided sewing machine method. It's been wonderful to achieve evenly laid stitches by simply pressing a button on the embroidery machine!

For many years, I created appliqués in books so readers could trace and prepare drawings for hand-guided sewing machine appliqué projects. Now my drawings have been digitized by Amazing Designs, Cactus Punch, and Husqvarna Viking and developed for use on an embroidery machine (refer to Chapter 5 for project inspiration). The CD-ROM included with this book has 20 new design concepts. I thought it would be fun to develop a fresh approach to finishing appliqué raw edges different from traditional satin stitches. You'll find specialty stitches that creatively cover the appliqué fabric raw edges and unique borders that frame some of the designs. Some stitches even look like fancy sewing machine stitches! I'll show you how to appliqué using creative techniques, such as dimensional, texture, and design combinations with a variety of fabrics beyond traditional cotton. For even more creativity, don't hesitate to mix some of the design segments with other appliqué designs you own.

All of the techniques and designs can be completed on your embroidery machine without additional software—but you can always use embroidery software to make the most of your appliqué creations.

Be adventurous and have fun!

Mary Mulari

Chapter 1

Frame an appliqué design with additional fabrics, trims, and decorative stitching to create a large, prominent focal point. The swirl appliqué design was embroidered on purple fabric with a raw edge appliqué for the center square. A button with a swirl pattern was sewn in the center. The purple fabric edges were turned under and stitched off center using decorative sewing machine stitches. Fusible bias tape was used to frame the purple square. For best results, place a piece of tear-away stabilizer beneath the sweatshirt to support the decorative stitches.

Appliqué Essentials

This traditional appliqué features a satin stitch edge finish.

Appliqué designs are perhaps the most popular design style for embroidery. They're quick to stitch and save time at the embroidery machine, allowing more time for creating fabulous projects! Appliqué areas in a design are often digitized to replace large fill stitch areas and to reduce a design's overall stitch count.

Design Choices

You'll find appliqué designs at your local sewing and embroidery machine dealer and Web sites of professional digitizing companies or individuals. To help you get started, there are 20 appliqué designs featured on the CD-ROM inside the back cover. A computer and perhaps compatible embroidery software will be required to access the designs. Determine what's needed for your embroidery machine by referring to the owner's manual or consulting the dealer honoring your warranty. The CD-ROM has folders for each embroidery machine file format.

Copy the design files onto a floppy disk, PC card, or the hard drive of your computer; or, open the designs directly into applicable embroidery software. Then, transfer the designs to your embroidery machine, following the manufacturer's instructions.

All 20 designs on the CD-ROM are ready to stitch as shown without adjustment in embroidery software. Three designs are included in both the standard 4" square and 5" x 7" formats. Depending on your embroidery machine capabilities, you may be able to reduce or enlarge the designs within the hoop to achieve greater flexibility. With additional embroidery software, you may enjoy making creative changes to the designs.

Most designs on the CD-ROM have unique appliqué edge stitches.

Design Segments

Appliqué designs are versatile. They all have segments or additional stops that offer a variety of techniques and creative design elements. These segments can be used individually or combined with other design elements to create new designs.

Each time the machine stops, a segment ends. Thread colors may not require changing. Select thread colors that match or contrast with your appliqué fabrics. The pre-set colors noted on the touch screen of your embroidery machine or in your software may not correspond with your fabric choices. I encourage you to change thread colors and use your own color coordinating creativity—even experiment using one thread color for an entire design. (Refer to page 30 for inspiration.)

For your convenience, details about the designs on the CD-ROM and their segments can be found on pages 44-47.

They are also printable from a PDF file on the CD-ROM. You'll find it easy to embroider the complete design or extract segments from the design using these pages as a guide.

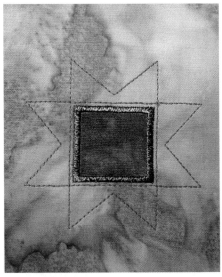

Forward through designs to find segments that can be used independently.

Mary Says — All appliqué designs pictured in chapters 1-4 are found on the CD-ROM inside the book's back cover.

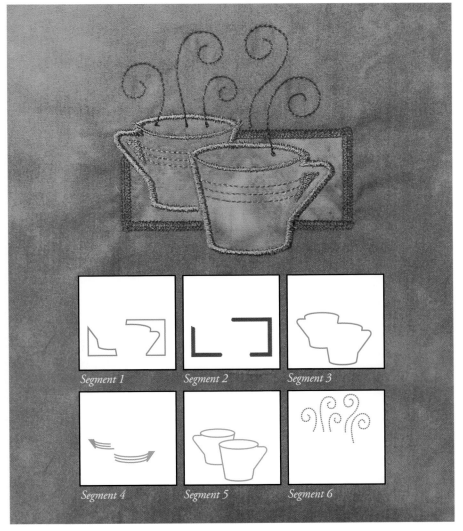

Segment 1   *Segment 2*   *Segment 3*

Segment 4   *Segment 5*   *Segment 6*

Coffee design and corresponding stitch segments.

Practice Stitch Samples

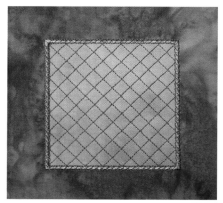

Test designs on fabric that is the same or similar to the project.

Use layers from silk flowers instead of a flower shape cut from fabric.

Practice stitch to make sure the placement of silk flower layers is just right for the flower center stitching.

It's smart to practice automatic appliqué on sample fabric before stitching designs directly on a garment or project. Practice stitching will build your confidence and skills, while creating a collection of stitch samples for use in future projects.

Make the most of your practice stitching efforts by choosing quality fabrics for the base and appliqués. I usually cut a 9" square of the base fabric and a corresponding piece of stabilizer for a standard size hoop. Test designs on the same or similar fabric as the project. The test will reveal whether you've chosen the correct stabilizer, thread, needle, and design.

Practice stitching also tests how fabric and thread colors blend or contrast. Experiment with new color combinations to take your appliqué experience to another level.

When you're ready to combine design segments or try echo appliqué, it's a great idea to practice stitch these techniques. You may be tempted to skip this "dress rehearsal" of appliqué, but you will have no regrets when the final production turns out just right.

Use practice stitch samples for patches and pockets. The leaves appliqué patch shown here is framed with two additional fabric patches.

Copyright

The designs included in this book are original and protected by the copyright laws. You may use the designs for personal use and for gifts or items to sell, but sharing, trading, or copying them is illegal. Please honor all copyrighted designs, and their designers, to encourage an on-going new supply of original designs for the future.

Embroidery Supplies

Successful "automatic appliqué" begins with using the correct supplies. This chapter details the basic information needed to create easy appliqués on the embroidery machine. For additional help and information, please refer to Jeanine Twigg's *Embroidery Machine Essentials* and *Companion Project Series: Basic Techniques*.

An assortment of threads range from small spools to large cones.

An assortment of hoop sizes help the embroidery process.

Stabilizers

The most commonly used stabilizers for appliqué designs are tear-away, cut-away, and water-soluble, depending on your base fabric. They are available in an assortment of weights and textures, but only a few colors. Your practice stitch samples will help you determine the appropriate stabilizer for each project.

Tear-away

Choose a light- to medium-weight tear-away stabilizers for woven fabrics. Care should be taken tearing away the stabilizer after the stitching is complete. Rather than ripping too vigorously and possibly damaging the stitching, firmly hold the fabric and finishing stitches with one hand while the other hand slowly pulls the stabilizer away from the stitching.

Cut-away

Choose a light- to medium-weight cut-away stabilizer for unstable fabrics, such as knits, fleece, and other fabrics that stretch. A cut-away stabilizer is used to support the stitching before, during, and after the embroidery process. To prevent stabilizer edges from showing on the right side of thin or sheer fabrics, trim the cut-away stabilizer with pinking or scalloping shears.

Water-soluble

Practice stitching appliqué designs on woven fabric with a single layer of water-soluble stabilizer. It may be necessary to use two or more layers to support the stitches. The stabilizer can be torn away from the outer edges (tear one layer away at a time), and then from inside the appliqué. Wet to dissolve any remaining stabilizer pieces. Use a single layer of water-soluble stabilizer as a topper on knit fabrics or fabrics with an uneven surface. When used as a topper, it will keep the stitches on the fabric top and prevent stitches from sinking into the fabric nap.

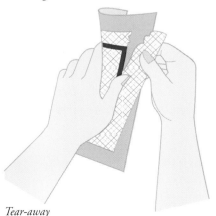

Tear-away

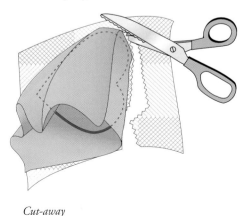

Cut-away

Mary Says Keep a supply of many different stabilizers on hand. When you find your favorite ones, buy them in large, economical rolls.

Appliqué Adhesives

It is important to secure the appliqué fabric to the base fabric prior to embroidering the raw edge finishing stitches. There are several ways to adhere an appliqué fabric to the base fabric. If an adhesive is not used, the appliqué fabric may shift during the embroidery process causing unwanted ripples or an uneven surface.

Temporary Spray Adhesives

Temporary spray adhesives do just what their name suggests—hold fabrics together for a short amount of time. The adhesive will dissipate with time or wash away during the laundry process. Use them to hold the appliqué fabric to the base fabric or to hold the base fabric to a hooped stabilizer.

Use the spray adhesive with care, in moderation, and in a ventilated area. Spray the back of the appliqué fabric lightly either inside a box or on an open newspaper to prevent overspray from landing on other surfaces or harming the embroidery machine. The spray adhesive makes the back of an appliqué fabric tacky so it will remain in place during the embroidery process. Without it, the appliqué fabric may shift causing ripples.

Fusible Adhesives

Adhesives that are used with the heat of a craft iron to secure to the back appliqué fabrics are available in a variety of styles. Fusible spray adhesive is an easy way to create a fusible appliqué. Using a box or newspaper for protection, spray the appliqué back with fusible adhesive. Allow the product to dry. Use this product according to the manufacturer's directions.

Paper-backed adhesive is available in two fusible styles—pressure sensitive and fusible web. For the pressure sensitive fusible, both sides of the adhesive have paper to protect the product. The standard fusible web has webbing on one side and paper on the other. To use, templates are drawn in reverse onto the paper, cut out and pressed or fused onto the hooped base fabric. A small craft iron and ironing surface are used to secure the layers together. For more information on this process, refer to page 18.

Mary Says Use a craft iron small enough to fit into a standard size hoop for securing appliqué fabric with fusible adhesive or web to the base fabric. Use a small padded ironing surface to work on when the hoop is removed from the machine.

Thread

Most embroidery designs are digitized for use with a 40-weight thread. Appliqué designs are no exception. But this doesn't mean that you can't experiment with other thread weights. The most common threads for appliqué are cotton, rayon, and polyester. Cotton threads provide a matte edge finish. Rayon and polyester provide a shiny edge finish. For items that will be washed frequently, polyester or acrylic threads are recommended. Rayon threads are best for items that are seldom laundered. Interesting edge finishes can be created with variegated, twisted, and metallic threads.

Threads with a lower weight number are thicker. It may be necessary to change the needle to a larger size and enlarge the design slightly to allow more space between the stitches. Threads with a higher weight number are thinner. It may be necessary to change the needle to a smaller size and reduce the design slightly to eliminate the potential for fabric showing through the stitches.

Use a variety of threads within a design to add interest.

Needles

Depending on the fabrics chosen for an appliqué project, the most commonly used needles are 75/11, 80/12, and 90/14. Match the needle size to the appliqué fabric and practice with the needle you plan to use. You will need to select a needle made specifically for stitching with metallic or specialty threads that sparkle and shine. When needed, select a needle made specifically for stitching with microfiber fabrics if you are stitching tightly woven fabrics.

When embroidering with thicker threads, use a needle with a larger eye, such as a topstitching needle. For thinner threads, use a standard size 75/11 needle made specifically for high-speed embroidery.

Mary Says

Change needles often. Successful appliqué stitching depends on a high quality needle that has not been overworked.

Scissors

The best scissors for appliqué are those with a turned up tip and sharp points for trimming away fabric and threads inside the embroidery hoop. Double curved scissors have been developed for use with hooped fabric. The curved handle is the perfect shape to clear the hoop edge while trimming appliqué fabric.

It is important to use curved tip scissors to lift appliqué fabric away from the base fabric while trimming. This will ensure that you don't cut into the base fabric and get a close cut next to the appliqué outline.

Interfacing

Interface lightweight fabrics for a smoother appliqué surface.

Some fabric, such as cotton and lightweight fabrics, are better for appliqué with a layer of lightweight fusible interfacing ironed on the back. An interfacing stabilizes the fabric raw edges and offers a smoother appliqué surface. One of my favorite interfacings is a tricot knit. Fuse the interfacing according to the manufacturer's instructions onto a piece of fabric larger than the appliqué outline. For knits or fabrics that stretch, secure the tricot fusible interfacing grain perpendicular to the fabric stretch for extra stability.

Mary Says

Use tape or an adhesive lint remover to lift loose threads off the base fabric after trimming.

Chapter 2

Add intense color and style to an ordinary scarf with an elegant appliqué. Silk dupioni fabrics and high sheen rayon threads complement the elegant, smooth surface of the faux cashmere scarf. Plan the design location for visibility when the scarf is worn.

Traditional Appliqué Techniques

Traditional satin stitches finish the appliqué raw edges.

Appliqué traditionally has satin stitch edge finishing stitches. The stitches form a smooth "cupped" edge over the fabric raw edge to prevent it from raveling. The edges can be shiny with rayon thread, matte with cotton thread, or full of color with variegated threads. Choices of fabric and threads are endless.

About Appliqué

The dictionary describes appliqué as the process of sewing one piece of fabric ornamentally to another. Through the ages, appliqué has been used as decoration on clothing and accessories for everyday living. It began as a handwork technique, and then moved to the sewing machine. Many of us learned to hand guide the sewing machine needle around the appliqué edge shapes using satin stitches. This is a sewing skill that takes practice and patience. Now we can use the embroidery machine's capabilities to produce perfectly guided appliqué stitches. Appliqué using an embroidery machine takes less time and thread than a traditional fill-stitch embroidery design as the appliqué fabric covers the stitch area instead.

The designs on the CD-ROM that accompany this book feature non-traditional appliqué edge finishes. The focus is to expand appliqué beyond traditional satin stitches, cotton fabrics, and basic techniques for more diverse creativity. Appliqué is still all about sewing one piece of fabric to another, but the creative variations are limitless.

Fabric Choices

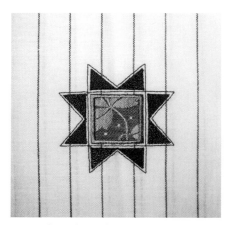

Solid color cotton fabrics are the traditional choice for appliqué, but it's more fun to dig deeper into your fabric collection to unearth a variety of unusual fabrics. If you are planning to wash your projects created with unusual fabric appliqués, be sure to test launder your fabric choices. As with any sewing project, prewash all fabrics to prevent shrinkage and to remove sizing that could interfere with the embroidery.

Choose appliqué and base fabrics that work together. For example, a thin silk base fabric will not support a heavy corduroy appliqué. Always test stitch, especially if you are uncertain about the selected item's compatibility. Use lightweight fusible interfacing on the appliqué fabric for added strength and stability if needed.

Here's a variety of basic fabrics to consider for appliqué: satin, sheers, velour, lamé, wool felt, velvet/velveteen, rayon, terrycloth, faux leather, flannel, faux suede, linen, taffeta, corduroy, lace, nylon organdy/organza, silk, mesh, interlock knits, fleece, and denim. Consider visiting a specialty fabric store for the most unique fabrics available.

Creatively combine fabric textures—even stripes and flowers go well in appliqué.

Fabric choices make a difference in each of these versions of the same design. Solid colors are usually a safe choice for appliqué but you may prefer to select fabrics with pattern or texture to add extra interest to a design. Experiment with new combinations like silk and terrycloth or faux suede and interlock knits. Your appliqués will no longer be ordinary!

Hooping

Most techniques and projects featured in this book involve hooping a base fabric with a stabilizer. To prevent design distortion, do not tug on the fabric or stabilizer once it is hooped. Hoop and unhoop to achieve the proper hoop tension by adjusting the hoop screw before the final hooping.

While trimming appliqué fabrics from inside the hoop, cut carefully and avoid pushing the scissor blades down on the hoped fabric. Use your non-cutting hand and fingers on the underside of the hoop to support the fabric and stabilizer in the area where you are trimming.

You may prefer to trim with the hoop on a clipboard. Practice holding the clipboard with one hand, and then trimming with the other. This method prevents loosening or distorting of the fabric and stabilizer layers.

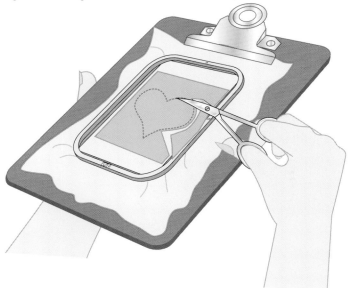

Mary Says

You may find it helpful to lift and hold the excess appliqué fabric off the base fabric with your non-cutting hand.

Mary Says

Clip-on magnifiers for eyeglasses can make the close trimming of appliqué fabrics easier. The magnifiers add bifocal strength to your reading or regular eyeglasses.

Some fabrics or projects should not be hooped due to the thickness, fabric stretch, or probability of hoop marks being left on the fabric. Instead hoop the stabilizer, spray it with temporary adhesive, and then secure the base fabric to the stabilizer. This will hold the layers in place during the embroidery process. For extra support, carefully pin the fabric on the inside hoop edges away from potential embroidery areas.

Stitch & Trim Appliqué

This quick and easy technique of appliqué is my favorite. It's neat and effortless with the perfect pair of curved tip embroidery scissors!

Variegated rayon thread creates a unique edge finish on this appliqué.

Instructions:

1. Hoop the base fabric with the appropriate stabilizer. Place the hoop on the embroidery machine and select the design to stitch. If this is your first time experimenting with an appliqué design, stitch the outline first. Restart the section with the outline to stitch again after the appliqué fabric placement. This will help you determine the exact location where the appliqué fabric should be placed.

2. Cut a piece of appliqué fabric slightly larger than the design shape. If uncertain about the size of the design, cut the fabric to fit inside the hoop. If the fabric is lightweight, fuse a layer of lightweight interfacing to the wrong side.

3. Lightly spray the back of the appliqué fabric with temporary adhesive (place it in a box for protection away from the machine) and fingerpress the appliqué fabric to the base fabric inside the hoop.

4. Stitch the appliqué outline portion of the design.

5. When the stitching is complete, remove the hoop from the machine but do not remove the fabric from the hoop. Trim the excess fabric away from the outline outer edge, leaving less than ¹⁄₁₆" of fabric beyond the stitching for best results.

6. Remove fabric across points if your design has sharp corners.

7. If you accidentally cut through stitches, it won't be a problem, as the next series of stitches will cover them. You will have more problems if the fabric edge beyond the outline is too wide. The extra threads poking out from behind the edge finishing stitches can be difficult or impossible to trim away after the appliqué is complete.

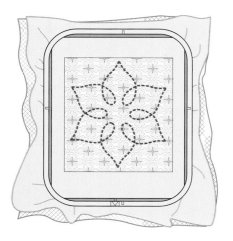

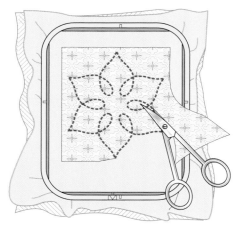

8. Return the hoop to the machine and stitch the remainder of the appliqué. There are usually a series of underlay stitches (zigzag) to help secure the fabric raw edges and to build a base for the satin stitches. Some decorative raw edge finishing stitches do not have underlay stitches, as the decorative stitches finish the raw edges and provide extra support.

9. Stop the machine just prior to the satin stitches to make sure all the fabric raw edges are close to the zigzag stitches.

Remove the hoop from the machine to perform additional trimming if necessary.

10. When the embroidery is complete, remove the hoop from the machine and then remove the base fabric and stabilizer from the hoop.

Note: To embroider with fleece as the appliqué fabric, refer to Jeanine Twigg's *Embroidery Machine Essentials: Fleece Techniques* by Nancy Cornwell. Nancy offers many unique appliqué tips and trick for embroidering with fleece!

Mary Says

To achieve professional looking appliqués, use a pair of very sharp, curved tip embroidery scissors and cut as closely as possible to the stitching line. Look at a ruler and the measure of 1/16". Leave less than this amount beyond the outline stitching.

Template Appliqué

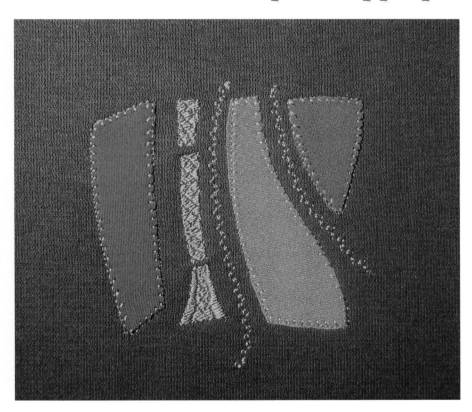

Use this technique to create exact size appliqué shapes and to avoid trimming excess fabric away from the base fabric inside the hoop. The shapes are stitched onto template material, cut out, and used to determine the exact shape of the appliqué fabric. This technique is perfect for blanket stitch edge finishes or appliqué designs that do not leave enough room between the outline and the satin stitch edge for trimming fabric. Be sure to use interesting fabrics with a variety of textures.

Instructions:

1. Place the inner and outer hoop sections together without fabric and tighten the tension screw.

2. Tape a 4"x 6" index card to the hoop back.

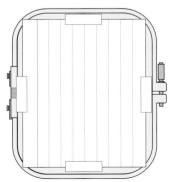

3. Attach the hoop to the machine. Without using thread in the needle, stitch the appliqué outline shape. If your machine has a sensor to detect an unthreaded needle, fool it by leaving the thread in the last thread guide above the needle and tape the thread to the machine.

4. Remove the hoop from the machine and the card from the hoop back. Using paper scissors cut the appliqué outline directly on the stitching holes in the card. This will be your template. Mark the template right side, or use lined index cards with the lined side as the appliqué template wrong side.

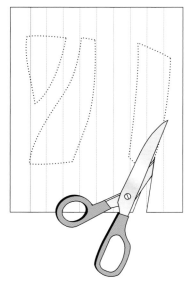

5. Trace the shape on the paper side of a piece of paper-backed fusible web or pressure sensitive adhesive, reversing the pattern. Cut out the template size.

6. Fuse the traced template onto the appliqué fabric wrong side. Cut out the appliqué shape following the lines drawn on the paper. Peel off the paper backing.

7. Hoop the base fabric with an appropriate stabilizer. Attach the hoop to the machine. Thread the machine and stitch the design outline again.

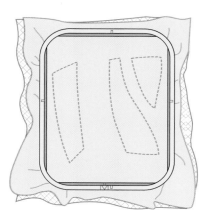

8. Remove the hoop from the machine; do not remove the fabric from the hoop. On a padded ironing surface, secure the appliqué shapes just inside the outline by finger pressing and using a craft iron to secure the layers together.

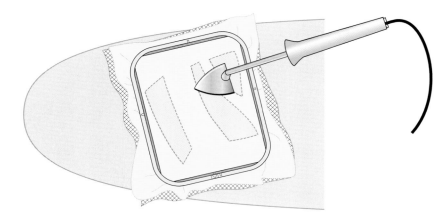

9. Return the hoop to the machine and complete the design.

10. When the embroidery is complete, remove the hoop from the machine, and then remove the base fabric and stabilizer from the hoop.

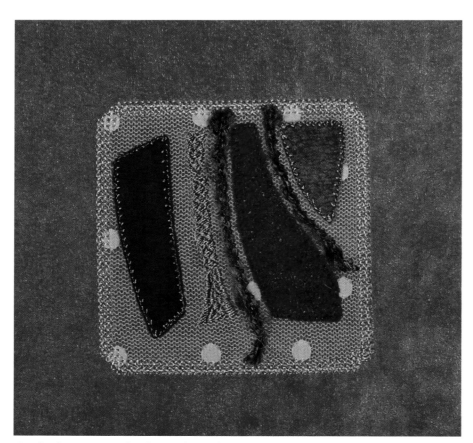

For the ultimate in mixed media, use the template method to couch over decorative threads, use lace as a base appliqué, mix fabric fibers, and just have fun mixing and matching.

Reverse Appliqué

Instead of trimming away the excess appliqué fabric outside the outline, the base fabric will be trimmed away to reveal the appliqué fabric beneath. Consider using lightweight fusible interfacing on the appliqué fabric back for extra stability.

On this sample, the purple fabric is the base fabric. After the entire design was stitched, I trimmed away most of the purple fabric, leaving only ½" beyond the border stitching, and pinked the edges.

Instructions

1. Hoop the fabrics with the appliqué fabric sandwiched between the base fabric and the stabilizer.

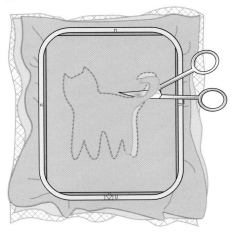

2. Place the hoop on the machine and stitch the design outline twice by stitching the outline and then starting the design over. Remove the hoop from the machine but do not remove the fabric from the hoop. Make a small cut through the base fabric only in the outline center. Do not cut into the appliqué fabric beneath. Trim away the base fabric from <u>inside</u> the design to expose the appliqué fabric.

3. Place the hoop back on the machine and embroider the raw edge finishing stitches.

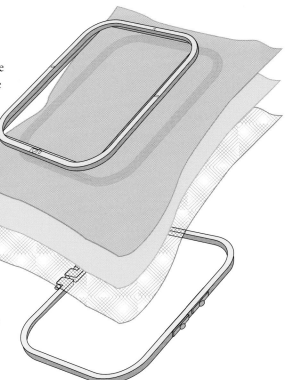

Chapter 3

Combine elements of two designs to create the floral display on the tote. The wavy satin stitch frame was stitched on-point on fabric that was made into the tote. Beads add extra interest to the frame. The floral center detail was created from another design element. Faux suede was embroidered on tear-away stabilizer and the floral shape was cut from the fabric. A piece of quilt batting behind the flower lifts it above the tote's surface.

Creative Appliqué Techniques

This chapter goes beyond the basics and traditional approaches of appliqué. Now you have lots of options and choices. As you see on this floral design, appliqué can be three dimensional instead of flat. Designs can be assembled from pieced or sheer fabrics, and their edges can be frayed or free of stitching. Study the designs with this book and look for segments to combine, shapes to pad, and new ways to use each design.

Allover Stitch Appliqué

Secure scrap pieces of appliqué fabrics to a base fabric with the use of decorative allover embroidery stitching.

Instructions:

1. Hoop the base fabric with the appropriate stabilizer.

2. Cut scraps of fabric or faux suede into small elongated shapes.

3. Select a design with allover stitching and thread to match the base fabric.

4. Place the hoop on the embroidery machine. Stitch the appliqué outline. This will serve as a placement guide for the pieces.

Wave Top Bag from *Made for Travel* by Mary Mulari

5. Remove the hoop from the machine, but do not remove the fabric from the hoop. Spray the back of scrap appliqué pieces with temporary adhesive (place it in a box for protection away from the machine). Position the pieces inside the design outline. For a free-form look to the design, allow the fabric edges to extend beyond the outline.

6. Return the hoop to the machine and continue embroidering. The allover stitch pattern will secure the appliqué fabrics to the base fabric. The fabrics will be firmly attached, but unlike traditional appliqué all the edges are not secure. If the fabrics fray, the design will have extra texture after laundering.

Cotton heart under allover stitches.

Velvet heart under allover stitches.

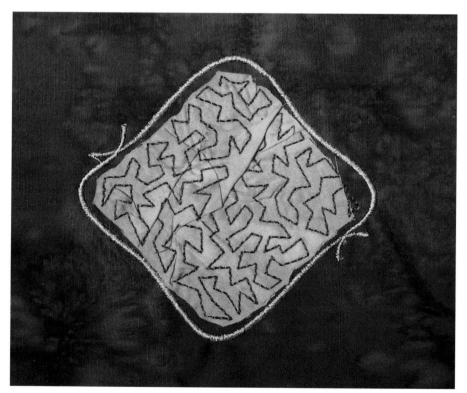

For an appliqué with a wrinkled, textured surface, liberally spray the back of lightweight fabric with temporary spray adhesive. The tacky surface will make it easy to create folds and wrinkles in the fabric as you fit it inside the outline.

Ribbon strips peaking out from under allover stitches.

Raw-Edge Appliqué

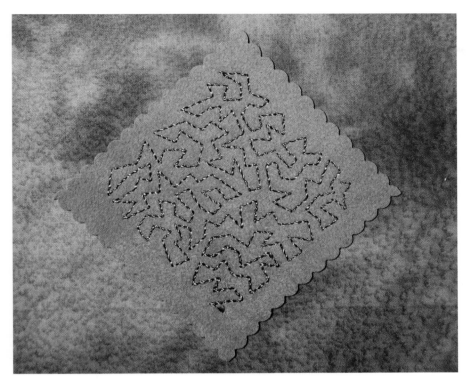

Faux suede appliqué stitched with twisted rayon thread.

Use this technique with fabrics that do not ravel, such as faux suede, felt, fleece, or vinyl. It is also great for use with paper to create cards, pictures, or scrapbook details.

Instructions:

1. Hoop the base fabric along with the appropriate stabilizer.

2. Cut a piece of appliqué fabric larger than the design shape and secure it to the hooped base fabric by spraying the back with temporary adhesive. Place the hoop on the embroidery machine and select the design to embroider.

3. Stitch the appliqué outline; repeat if necessary.

4. Remove the hoop from the machine and trim away the excess fabric from outside the stitching line. Use the curved tip embroidery scissors to trim close to the outline or use pinking shears for a wider edge around the appliqué.

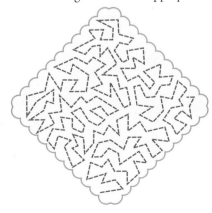

Use this technique on paper by taping the paper and a piece of tear- or cut-away stabilizer to the hoop back. Make sure it is taped securely. Embroider the design similarly to the template-making method on pages 17 and 18.

Frayed-Edge Appliqué

For interesting dimension, select fabrics that will fray when laundered, such as cotton, homespun, silk, satin, linen, denim, and flannel. Make sure to cut the appliqué fabric pieces larger than the design by more than ½" around.

Instructions:

1. Hoop the base fabric along with the appropriate stabilizer.

2. Cut a piece of appliqué fabric as large as the hoop embroidery area.

3. Position the appliqué fabric (with temporary spray adhesive) onto the base fabric.

4. Place the hoop on the embroidery machine and select the design to embroider.

5. Stitch the appliqué outline and the finishing stitches.

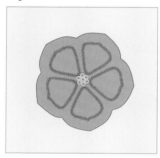

6. Remove the hoop from the machine. Keep the fabric in the hoop while trimming the excess fabric from around the stitching, leaving ½" all around, or a varying width.

7. Snip into the raw edge around the design.

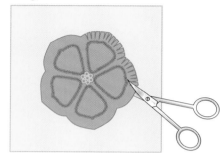

8. Remove the fabrics from the hoop and launder the piece to create the frayed raw edge. Or, brush the snipped edges with an old toothbrush or a small wire brush.

Allow raw edges to ravel even more on natural fabrics such as silk (above) or linen (below).

Appliqué flower stitched on heavyweight denim from worn blue jeans.

Liberated Appliqué

Cut appliqués loose and turn them into freestanding elements. Appliqué designs are embroidered onto a base of water-soluble stabilizer or sheer fabric.

Water-Soluble Base

Instructions:

1. Hoop two layers of regular weight water-soluble stabilizer or one layer of heavyweight.

2. Cut out appliqué fabric and apply a layer of lightweight interfacing to the wrong side. Spray the back with temporary spray adhesive (place it in a box for protection away from the machine) and position it on the hooped stabilizer.

3. Place the hoop on the embroidery machine and select the design to embroider.

4. Stitch the design outline, trim away excess fabric, and complete the stitching.

5. Remove the design and stabilizer from the hoop. Tear away the stabilizer layers one at a time. If pieces of stabilizer remain on the edge, lightly wet the design edges to dissolve the stabilizer. Allow the design to dry.

6. Sew the design onto a garment or piece of fabric by zigzag stitching over the edge stitching with matching thread.

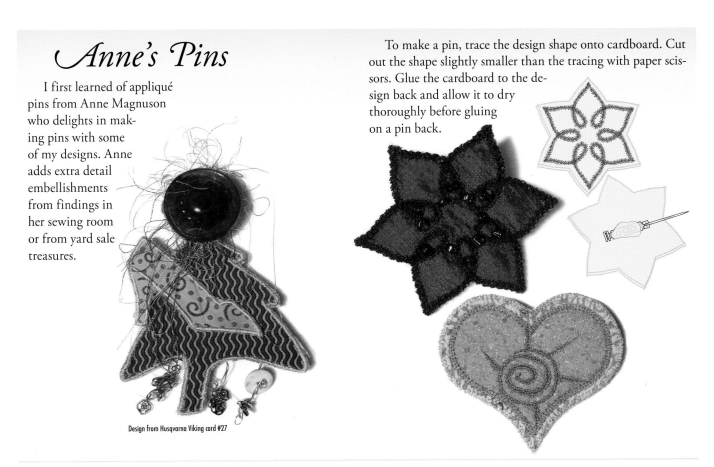

Anne's Pins

I first learned of appliqué pins from Anne Magnuson who delights in making pins with some of my designs. Anne adds extra detail embellishments from findings in her sewing room or from yard sale treasures.

To make a pin, trace the design shape onto cardboard. Cut out the shape slightly smaller than the tracing with paper scissors. Glue the cardboard to the design back and allow it to dry thoroughly before gluing on a pin back.

Design from Husqvarna Viking card #27

Sheer Fabric Base

To create liberated appliqués with a sheer base, such as organza or organdy, you will need a hot knife, stencil cutter, or wood-burning tool and a design with smooth edge finishing stitches. Choose a fabric-edge melting tool with a low temperature, such as a 9 to 15 watt, to prevent sheer thread and fabric edges from burning.

Instructions:

1. Hoop two layers of organza or one layer of organdy. As a backing, these fabrics give body to the appliqué and will be left in place after the embroidery is complete.

2. Spray the appliqué fabric back with temporary spray before finger pressing it to the hooped fabric.

3. Place the hoop on the embroidery machine and select the design to embroider.

4. Stitch the appliqué outline, trim away the excess fabric, and embroider the edge finishing stitches.

5. Remove the fabric from the hoop and trim it away close to the outer stitched edge. Heat the fabric-edge melting tool. Gently press and move the heated end over the fabric to melt away the excess raw fabric edges. Be careful not to hold the tool in place as it will burn or scorch the edges.

Padded Appliqué

Add dimension to appliqué designs by inserting a layer of quilt batting to create a raised surface. For even more dimension, cut a second layer of batting smaller than the first and lay it underneath it.

1. Using the template technique on page 17, make an index card pattern of the design you plan to pad with batting.

2. Hoop the base fabric with the appropriate stabilizer.

3. Place the hoop on the embroidery machine and select the design to embroider.

4. Stitch the design outline on the base fabric.

5. Remove the hoop from the machine; do not remove the fabric from the hoop.

6. Use the template pattern to cut a layer of quilt batting ¼" smaller than the design. Spray the batting back with temporary adhesive and position it inside the stitched outline.

7. Spray the appliqué fabric back with temporary adhesive and place it over the appliqué outline and batting.

8. Stitch the outline again. Remove the hoop from the machine but keep the fabric in the hoop. Trim away the excess appliqué fabric outside the stitching line.

9. Return the hoop to the machine and complete the design.

Dimensional Appliqué

Break tradition by sewing appliqués in place in new ways and lifting the edges from the surface of the base fabric.

1. Make a paper template of the leaf shapes, or a design of your choice, using the instructions on page 17. Cut the design shapes from non-fray fabrics such as faux suede, felt, or vinyl.

2. Hoop the base fabric with the appropriate stabilizer, place the hoop on the embroidery machine, and select the design to embroider.

3. Stitch the outlines of the design shapes with thread that matches the base fabric for a less noticeable stitching line.

4. Use temporary fusible spray on the backs of the appliqué design shapes to position and hold the design shapes inside the outlined areas. For the leaf design, continue with the branch and vein stitching, which secures the designs to the fabric base.

5. For the flowers featured on the hat, sew the flower outline on hooped tear-away stabilizer instead of a base fabric. Embroider the center detail after the flower shapes have been set into position within the stitching outline on the stabilizer. Remove the stabilizer from the back of the flowers and pin or hand stitch the flowers to the hat.

Mary Says
Use the dimensional appliqué technique on tear-away stabilizer to produce a collection of designs to arrange and stitch on a garment. This makes it easy to add appliqués to hard to hoop areas of ready-made clothing.

Combine dimensional techniques as I've done with this design. Instead of being stitched on as the last segment of this framed design, the leaf is completed as a separate piece and pinned or hand stitched in place.

Hoop a layer of sheer fabric, cut a piece of thin batting smaller than the appliqué shape, and embroider on appliqué fabric following the padded appliqué method on the previous page. Melt off the sheer fabric backing edges with the fabric-edge melting tool.

Sheer & Lace Appliqué

Create a see-through effect with sheer or lace as the appliqué fabric. Use a stabilizer—light or dark—to blend with the base fabric. When selecting lace, consider the pattern. Spaces or holes between the threads can affect the end result.

Instructions

1. Hoop the base fabric with the appropriate stabilizer.

2. Cut a piece of sheer or lace fabric for the appliqué, spray the back with temporary adhesive spray, and position it inside the hoop.

3. Place the hoop on the embroidery machine and select the design to embroider.

4. Stitch the design outline twice.

5. Remove the hoop from the machine; do not remove the fabric from the hoop. Trim away the excess fabric around the outline. Cut delicate fabrics slowly and carefully. It's easy to catch the scissor tips in the lace holes.

6. Return the hoop to the machine to complete the design embroidery.

Mix sheer fabric with lace for a delightfully dainty appliqué.

Textured Appliqué

Make appliqués more interesting by adding decorative machine stitches to the appliqué fabric. Thread colors that match the fabric create subtle texture while threads that contrast with the fabric color add more obvious embellishment.

1. Use decorative stitches on the sewing machine to texturize the appliqué fabric. Simply stitch parallel or perpendicular rows using a variety of stitches or the same one over the entire surface. For best results, interface the fabric before adding decorative stitches.

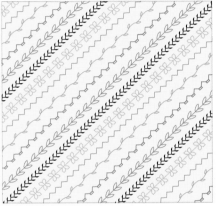

2. Hoop the base fabric with the appropriate stabilizer.

3. Position the embellished fabric onto the base fabric.

4. Place the hoop on the embroidery machine and select the design to embroider.

5. Stitch the appliqué outline. Remove the hoop from the machine; do not remove the fabric from the hoop.

6. Trim the excess fabric surrounding the outline.

7. Return the hoop to the machine and finish the design.

Mary Says

Embroider your appliqué fabric with texturizing stitches by using one segment from a design on the CD-ROM. Hoop your project base fabric with the appropriate stabilizer and use embroidered appliqué fabric within another design.

The cross hatch stitching pattern adds texture to fabric. Use the fabric for the top square layer of the fern design on page 28, or the cat, quilt block, or star designs.

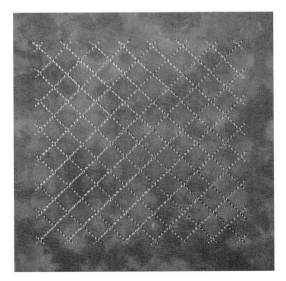

Echo Appliqué

An extra row of stitching beyond the outer edge of a design is called echo stitching. For fun, I've added echo decorative stitches to several designs on the CD-ROM, but you can add this detail to other designs as well.

Select a design and do a test stitching before working on the final project. Make notes on the adjustments you make as you reduce and enlarge the size of the design.

Reduce the size of the appliqué and stitch the design. Then enlarge the design to its maximum size and stitch the outline stitching around the edges of the appliqué. Use a different thread color for the echo stitching, as I did with the star design shown. You can also combine this stitching idea with Fabricless Appliqué below

Echo stitching adds dimension to appliqué.

Fabricless Appliqué

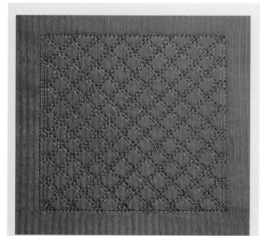

Use a double needle for added creativity.

Expand the use of appliqué designs by skipping the use of fabric—use only the embroidery stitches as an embellishment. This technique is certainly a time saver as no fabric placement and trimming is required. Simply let the embroidery machine sew. You can even turn off the "stops" on some machines or keep pressing "start" when the machine stops for using all one thread color. This technique offers a quick-to-stitch variety.

Or, stitch only the appliqué outline with a double needle to see the effect created. Use a 2.0 double needle on light- to medium-weight fabrics.

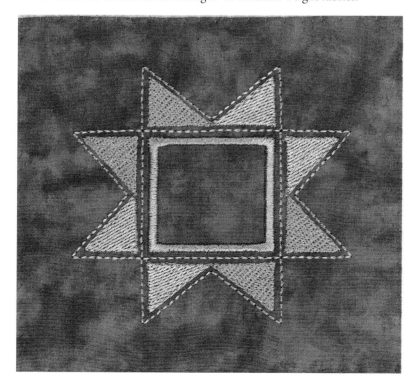

Patchwork Appliqué

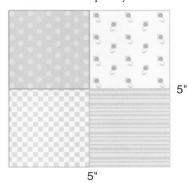

Piece four fabrics together before using it for an appliqué. Use this technique for the star design featured on the CD-ROM.

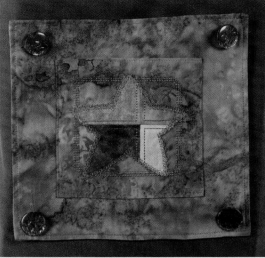

Trim the appliqué base fabric to a 5" square and turn under the edges ¼". Sew to an 8" square of fabric. Cut another 8" square for the backing, sew the two layers together and turn right side out. Attach the square to the bag with shank buttons at each corner.

Instructions

1. Piece together four 2½" squares of fabric, using a short stitch length. If the fabrics are thin cottons, fuse a layer of lightweight fusible interfacing on the patch wrong side after piecing. Spray the patch back with temporary adhesive.

2. Hoop the base fabric with the appropriate stabilizer.

3. Place the hoop on the embroidery machine and select the design to embroider.

4. The first segment is the intersection lines for the pieced appliqué placement.

5. Place the seamlines of the patchwork in line with the stitching on the base fabric. Stitch the outline around the star.

6. Remove the hoop from the machine; do not remove the fabrics from the hoop.

7. Trim the excess fabric from around the star outline.

8. Return the hoop to the machine and complete the remaining design.

5"

5"

Chapter 4

Create a wallhanging with practice stitch samples appliquéd onto textured fabric. Select three compatible samples or stitch them with a plan and color theme in mind. Turn under the edges of the stitched patches and sew them on the base fabric with clear monofilament thread. The patches could also be sewn on as pockets. Use additional matching pieces of fabric for the rod casings.

Appliqué Accents

Don't stop just because the embroidery machine does! It's OK and even advisable to skip segments of designs just so you can add something interesting to an appliqué. Use your collection of trims, buttons, beads, and curiosities to make appliqués dimensional, eye-catching, and spectacular. This is what's called adding your own designer touch to the designs.

Hand sew buttons to an embroidery design in place of flowers for a fun accent.

Beads, Bangles & Buttons

Mary Says

Use an appliqué as a foundation for a color-coordinated piece of jewelry.

The silk fabric I used for this appliqué pin is very elegant, but I liked adding a few beads to highlight the center and add some shine.

Hand sew beads in the center of flowers for added dimension.

Movable Appliqué

Use geometric design shapes for a collection of button trims that can be moved from one garment to another.

1. To make seven button trims, fuse lightweight interfacing to the appliqué fabric's wrong side.

2. Hoop two layers of water-soluble stabilizer.

3. Place the hoop on the embroidery machine and select the design to embroider.

4. Place the appliqué fabrics one at a time over each geometric shape area. Embroider the outline around each area, using the "Design Details" on page 44.

5. Remove the hoop from the machine; do not remove the fabric from the hoop. Trim the excess fabric away from the outlines.

6. Return the hoop to the machine to continue stitching the design. Embroider the buttonhole in each shape center.

7. After the stitching is completed for each shape, remove the hoop from the machine and carefully tear the stabilizer layers away from the seven shapes. Cut the buttonholes open and button each shape over the buttons on a shirt.

The design can also be used independently as a pocket decoration. Do not open the buttonholes; hand sew buttons over the buttonholes.

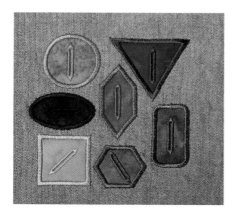

Button a framed design on an apron. Select shank buttons, one for each corner, and pin through the apron back to hold both the buttons and the design in place.

Appliqués as Luggage Tags

Make a luggage tag as a liberated appliqué from the large "Bon Voyage" design from the CD-ROM. A large tag in brightly colored fabric will make it easy to spot your suitcase on an airport luggage carousel. You'll need a of clear vinyl 5½" square along with standard appliqué supplies.

Instructions:

1. On hooped water-soluble stabilizer, layer a piece of appliqué (tag) fabric wrong side up, a layer of crisp interfacing or fusible fleece, and another piece of appliqué fabric for the tag top, right side up. Hold all layers in place with temporary spray adhesive.

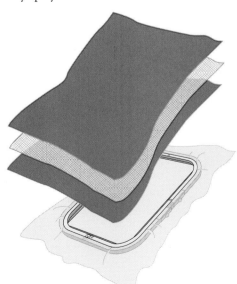

2. Place the hoop on the embroidery machine and select the design to stitch.

3. Use matching needle and bobbin threads for the edges and hole outline. Use a contrasting top thread color for the "Bon Voyage" lettering with bobbin thread to match the tag fabric.

4. Trim away the fabric inside the hole before satin stitching the edges. Do not stitch the cord as it is the last design segment and unnecessary for this project.

5. After the embroidery is complete, remove the fabric and stabilizer from the hoop. Tear the stabilizer away from the edges and tag center back.

6. Position the 5½" square piece of vinyl over the tag back, using clear tape to hold it in place.

7. Zigzag stitch the vinyl edges with clear nylon thread and bobbin thread to match the tag edges. A Teflon presser foot will make it easier to sew on vinyl. If necessary, trim the vinyl edges to the tag size; avoid trimming the satin stitches.

8. Insert a business card or a bag owner's identification in the vinyl pocket and use a piece of ribbon or cord to tie the tag to a suitcase.

Patches and Pockets

Create a pocket from practice stitch samples.

When I began stitching appliqué designs on the embroidery machine, I was hesitant to stitch designs directly onto a garment. I was unsure of placement and whether I could hoop the fabric straight. So instead, I created patches and pockets. This continues to be my favorite way to decorate with appliqué designs and it takes the worry out of placement.

Patches

Use a clear quilting ruler, such as a square, to center the design and determine the boundaries of your embroidered fabric piece. Cut 4" square standard size designs an inch larger. Turn under the raw edges ¼" and sew the patch in position with a satin stitch or another decorative sewing machine stitch.

You can also enlarge and frame the square by sewing fabrics to the outer edges. When cutting fabric strips for the outer edges, don't forget about the extra width for seam allowances and turning under the raw edges.

Pockets

Make a pocket by centering or offsetting the appliqué design on the fabric. Allow for ¼" side and bottom seam allowances and a wider allowance (approximately 1") for the top edge. Turn under and press the seam allowances and stitch the appliquéd pocket to its location.

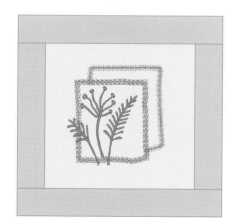

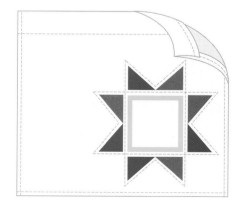

Frames for Appliqué

Emphasize a design with a stitched frame.

Many appliqués become more interesting and noticeable with an embroidered frame. There are several designs with frames on the CD-ROM. They can be mixed and matched with different designs from the book or with other designs you have in your collection.

The frames are also appliqué shapes. They can outline a photo printed on special fabric or stitched as an enclosure for a piece of jewelry, a button collection, or other decorations. (Photo: Mary & Rita in Sweden)

Combining Designs

Mary Says Study the segments of each design for ideas and ways to combine portions of several designs. Challenge yourself to go within the designs to find stitch segments that can be used alone, enlarged or reduced, or enhanced with part of a different design.

Combine designs and techniques. The petals were stitched in reverse appliqué and the flower center is from another design.

Several designs on the CD-ROM have frames built in. Use the frame designs with elements other than the one digitized with the design.

When you select a frame or background pattern, you may need to enlarge or reduce it plus or minus 20 percent on your machine or embroidery software. For example, enlarge a frame and reduce the new center image. Always embroider the frame first to ensure the center design will fit within the frame boundaries. Test stitching is recommended.

With some embroidery machines, it may be quicker to experiment with design sizing using embroidery software. The computer monitor is larger and can produce closer (zoom) viewing of design combinations. Save new files and transfer the designs to your embroidery machine.

An allover stitch pattern is combined with fern stitching from another design for this pocket embellishment.

Chapter 5

Use your collection of practice samples to create a quilt with designs all from a favorite card or design disk pack. Use similar fabrics for the appliqués as well as the sashing and borders. Determine the smallest sample size and trim all sample pieces to match. Or, choose a size appropriate for the fabric sizes to fit the chosen quilt pattern. Piece the practice samples together with color coordinating sashing strips and borders. Tie the quilt layers together with decorative buttons.

Gallery of Project Ideas

This chapter showcases a gallery of creative ideas and inspiration for using your collection of appliqué designs. Use "automatic appliqué" on ready-made garments and accessories, or creations you've sewn from scratch.

Even if I'm just testing a design, I always make sure to use interesting and colorful quality fabrics. The practice pieces eventually become part of a project. I encourage you to build a collection of practice samples, as they'll be readily available to create quick gifts by simply adding a few more minutes of sewing time. The projects in this chapter were created from my collection of Husqvarna Viking, Amazing Designs, and Cactus Punch design disks and cards.

Use practice samples with similar themes. The three appliqué patches on this sample all have a nature theme. Two tan square background fabrics are the same, but the stripes run horizontally on the fish appliqué. The finished square sizes are 4" with each edge turned under ¼". There are many decorative machine choices for sewing the squares to the shirt. I chose a feather stitch sewn with a medium-tan color thread. For a less obvious stitching line, use clear nylon sewing thread and a narrow zigzag stitch or straight stitch. (Designs from Cactus Punch card #20.)

Make one small appliqué design stand out with the addition of fabric frames and embellishments. Two complementary fabrics are layered beneath the original appliqué design. Two trim strips and three buttons were used for additional embellishment. The middle fabric frame layer is purposely positioned crooked as it extends over the lower frame edge. The appliqué design, was stitched on a 9" fabric square and trimmed in size to 4½" x 5". The raw edges were turned under ¼" for a clean finish. Use a sewing machine decorative blanket stitch to secure the patch to the other fabrics. (Design from Husqvarna Viking card #27.)

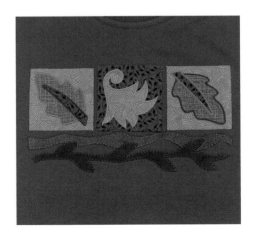

A trio of leaf designs trims this sample. Two designs are the same, but placed in opposite directions. Two pieces of Ultrasuede are blanket stitched beneath the design squares as an accent. It was easier for me to build this ensemble by working with appliqué patches rather than trying to sew the designs directly to the sample. This way I could position all the elements before the final securing stitches. (Design from Husqvarna Viking card #27.)

It's easy to make Christmas ornaments from appliqué designs. The embroidered square was cut from the base fabric "on point." Piping, hanging loop, and tassel were added, and then sewn to another square of fabric of the same size (approximately 4½"). An opening was left open for stuffing and then hand sewn closed. A button was added to the ornament bottom point to cover the "not-so-neat" piping overlap. (Design from Amazing Designs card #3005.)

Created as a backdoor wallhanging, the pockets feature appliqué designs. The base fabric has a subtle pattern that offers an interesting texture behind each appliqué. Solid green squares frame and set off each pocket on a single layer of faux suede fabric. This wallhanging was quick to assemble after stitching the appliqués and is decorative as well as functional.
(Designs from Amazing Designs card #3015.)

This special occasion purse is from my book *Accessories with Style*. The purse flap can be decorated in so many ways—"automatic appliqué" being my favorite. The appliqué design on the purse top flap is positioned off center intentionally as this planned placement adds an artistic touch to both the purse and the appliqué. (Design from Amazing Designs card #3008.)

One of the fastest and easiest gifts to make is a decorated kitchen towel. I keep a good supply of extra towels on hand for gift giving. This sample has an extra sewn fabric band across the towel lower edge width. The square featuring the tree appliqué is stitched above the band. The fabric was turned under a ¼", and then stitched to the towel. Plan to trim a towel for your friend's kitchen color scheme or for a special December holiday as every kitchen can use a new towel. (Designs from Amazing Designs card #3005.)

Tote bags are always a great gift. This tote features layered pockets with a small appliquéd pocket for storing tickets or keys. Rotating the pocket makes the entire tote more eye-catching. I love the look of natural colored linen, so it's often my choice for the base fabric. (Design from Husqvarna Viking card #27.)

Eleven appliqué patches, all created with red and green Christmas colors, are stitched to this purchased Christmas tree skirt. Some of the designs are not related to the holiday season, but the colors of fabric and thread coordinate to build the theme. Clear nylon thread was used to sew the turned under patch edges to the skirt. Buttons were sewn to the skirt, as extra design accents. (Design from Husqvarna Viking card #27.)

It's so easy to wavy cut and fringe a scarf from a ¼ yard of fleece. Decorate it with multiple appliqué designs from your collection. The flannel shapes were stitched on water-soluble stabilizer using directions similar to those used for Liberated Appliqué on page 25. Zigzag sewing machine stitches were used to secure the patches to the scarf. (Design from Husqvarna Viking card #27.)

Designs can be appliquéd directly to a variety of fabrics and accessories including scarves. Instead of hooping the scarf, hoop a piece of water-soluble stabilizer and use temporary spray adhesive to secure the scarf on the stabilizer. Be sure to match the bobbin thread color to the needle thread color as both sides will be visible when the scarf is worn. I like to randomly stitch a few appliqués design on a scarf, using a thin organdy or chiffon for the appliqués so the scarf doesn't become stiff with added fabric. (Design from Cactus Punch card #20.)

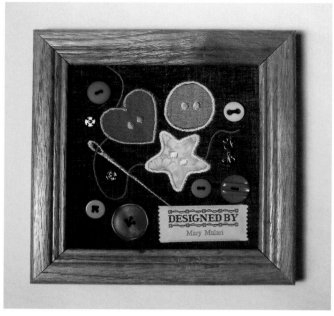

Here's a sewing room framed accent created with an appliqué design, and then embellished with sewing notions and trims. Choose any standard-size appliqué design to frame in a 5" square frame. With the right fabric colors and design choices, this framed ensemble will be a reminder of your creativity.

(Design from Husqvarna Viking card #27.)

A layer of fabric beneath appliqué fabric samples is a creative way to build a larger project. This concept is perfect for the pockets on this holiday greeting card storage wallhanging. Metallic threads add sparkle to the appliqué designs and decorative machine stitches were chosen for sewing the designs to the fabrics and pockets.

(Design from Husqvarna Viking card #27.)

Appliqués are great additions to this fabric pocket necklace, a project from my book *Accessories with Style*. The necklaces are also reversible so each side can feature a different appliqué. Cords in the side casings slide to make the necklace lengths adjustable.

(Design from Husqvarna Viking card #27.)

Stitch appliqués near the center of an 18" length of 6" wide lace, sew up the sides, turn right sides out, and you'll have a bag for sachet, soap, or potpourri. I chose elegant sheer and rayon fabrics for the appliqués with decorative ribbons to match.

(Designs from Husqvarna Viking card #27.)

Resources

Look for these and other embroidery products at a local retailer where embroidery machines, software, and designs are sold. To find a dealer near you, contact these companies of interest.

Designs and Supplies

Amazing Designs
(800) 443-8752
www.amazingdesigns.com

Cactus Punch
(800) 487-6972
www.cactuspunch.com

Dakota Collectibles
(800) 308-5442
www.dakotacollectibles.com

Embroideryarts
(888) 238-1372
www.embroideryarts.com

Mary's Productions (Mary Mulari)
(218) 229-2804
www.marymulari.com

Nancy's Notions
(800) 833-0690
www.nancynotions.com

Oklahoma Embroidery Supply & Design (OESD)
(800) 580-8885
www.embroideryonline.com

Embroidery Publications

Creative Machine Embroidery
(800) 677-5212
www.cmemag.com

Designs in Machine Embroidery
(888) SEW-0555
www.dzgns.com

Embroidery Journal
(480) 419-0167
www.embroideryjournal.com

Sew News
(800) 289-6397
www.sewnews.com

Embroidery Machine Companies

Baby Lock
(800) 422-2952
www.babylock.com

Bernina
(800) 405-2739
www.berninausa.com

Brother
(800) 422-7684
www.brother.com

Elna
(800) 848-3562
www.elnausa.com

Viking Sewing Machines
(800) 358-0001
www.husqvarnaviking.com

Janome
(800) 631-0183
www.janome.com

Kenmore
(888) 809-7158
www.sears.com

Pfaff
(800) 997-3233
www.pfaff.com

Simplicity
(800) 553-5332
www.simplicitysewing.com

Singer
(800) 474-6437
www.singershop.com

White
(800) 311-3164
www.whitesewing.com

Design Details

Abstract   Stitch Count: 3,086   Size: 3.33" x 3.47" (84.58mm x 88.14mm)

| Segment 1 | Segment 2 | Segment 3 | Segment 4 | Segment 5 | Segment 6 |

| Segment 7 | Segment 8 | Segment 9 |

Buttonholes & Shapes   Stitch Count: 7,116   Size: 3.86" x 3.78" (98.04mm x 96.01mm)

| Segment 1 | Segment 2 | Segment 3 | Segment 4 | Segment 5 | Segment 6 | Segment 7 |

| Segment 8 | Segment 9 | Segment 10 | Segment 11 | Segment 12 | Segment 13 | Segment 14 |

| Segment 15 | Segment 16 | Segment 17 | Segment 18 | Segment 19 | Segment 20 | Segment 21 |

Cat   Stitch Count: 4,570   Size: 3.86" x 3.75" (98.04mm x 95.25mm)

| Segment 1 | Segment 2 | Segment 3 | Segment 4 | Segment 4 |

Coffee Cups   Stitch Count: 4,866   Size: 3.36" x 3.40" (85.34mm x 86.36mm)

| Segment 1 | Segment 2 | Segment 3 | Segment 4 | Segment 5 | Segment 6 |

Crosshatch Frame   Stitch Count: 8,016   Size: 3.78" x 3.80" (96.0mm x 96.5mm)

| Segment 1 | Segment 2 | Segment 3 | Segment 4 | Segment 5 | Segment 6 |

Fern Patches (4")   Stitch Count: 5,048   Size: 3.27" x 3.28" (83.08mm x 83.31mm)

Segment 1   Segment 2   Segment 3   Segment 4   Segment 5

Fern Patches (5 x 7")   Stitch Count: 7,435   Size: 4.76" x 5.44" (120.90mm x 138.18mm)

Segment 1   Segment 2   Segment 3   Segment 4   Segment 5

Filigree Frame   Stitch Count: 7,604   Size: 3.87" x 3.75" (98.30mm x 95.25mm)

Segment 1   Segment 2   Segment 3   Segment 4   Segment 5

Flower Center   Stitch Count: 5,935   Size: 3.86" x 3.68" (98.04mm x 93.47mm)

Segment 1   Segment 2   Segment 3   Segment 4   Segment 4

Fringed Flower   Stitch Count: 4,911   Size: 3.86" x 3.86" (98.04mm x 98.04mm)

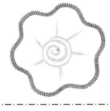

Segment 1   Segment 2   Segment 3

Heart   Stitch Count: 3,193   Size: 3.47" x 3.14" (88.14mm x 79.76mm)

Segment 1   Segment 2   Segment 3   Segment 4   Segment 5

Leaves   Stitch Count: 2,259   Size: 3.86" x 3.85" (98.04mm x 97.79mm)

Segment 1

Segment 2

Segment 3

Segment 4

Mary   Stitch Count: 7,116   Size: 3.86" x 3.86" (98.04mm x 98.04mm)

Segment 1

On Point (4")   Stitch Count: 3,926   Size: 3.83" x 3.76" (97.28mm x 95.50mm)
On Point (5" x 7")   Stitch Count: 4,934   Size: 4.83" x 4.74" (122.68mm x 120.40mm)

Segment 1

Segment 2

Segment 3
Segment 4

Plant in Pot   Stitch Count: 9,718   Size: 3.48" x 3.79" (88.39mm x 96.27mm)

Segment 1
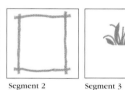
Segment 2

Segment 3

Segment 4

Segment 5

Segment 6

Segment 7

Quilt Block   Stitch Count: 5,771   Size: 3.29" x 3.29" (83.40mm x 83.40mm)

Segment 1

Segment 2

Segment 3

Segment 4

Segment 5

Quilt Swirl   Stitch Count: 6,571   Size: 3.82" x 3.88" (97.03mm x 98.55mm)

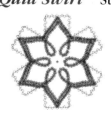

Segment 1

Segment 2

Segment 3

Segment 4

Segment 5

Segment 6

Red Hat Stitch Count: 7,885 Size: 3.86" x 3.86" (98.04mm x 98.04mm)

Segment 1   Segment 2   Segment 3   Segment 4   Segment 5   Segment 6   Segment 7

Star Stitch Count: 3,184 Size: 3.86" x 3.65" (98.04mm x 92.71mm)

Segment 1   Segment 2   Segment 3   Segment 4   Segment 5   Segment 6

Swirlies Stitch Count: 3,416 Size: 3.82" x 3.86" (97.03mm x 98.04mm)

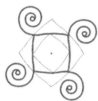

Segment 1   Segment 2

Tag (4") Stitch Count: 6,399 Size: 3.39" x 3.87" (86.11mm x 98.30mm)
Tag (5" x 7") Stitch Count: 11,391 Size: 5.73" x 6.54" (145.54mm x 166.12mm)

Segment 1   Segment 2   Segment 3   Segment 4   Segment 5   Segment 6

For more information on embroidery, purchase additional titles in this series: *Embroidery Machine Essentials, More Embroidery Machine Essentials, Companion Project Series: Basic Techniques, Companion Project Series: Fleece Techniques,* and *Companion Project Series: Quilting Techniques.*

CD-ROM Instructions

The embroidery designs featured in this book are located on the CD-ROM. You must have a computer and compatible embroidery software to access and utilize the decorative designs. Basic computer knowledge is helpful to understand how to copy the designs onto the hard-drive of your computer.

To access the designs, insert the CD-ROM into your computer. The designs are located on the CD-ROM in folders for each embroidery machine format. Copy the design files onto the computer hard-drive using one of the operating system (Windows) programs or open the design in applicable embroidery software. Be sure to copy only the design format compatible with your brand of embroidery equipment.

Once the designs are in your embroidery software or saved on your computer, transfer the designs to your embroidery machine following the manufacturer's instructions for your equipment. For more information about using these designs with your software or embroidery equipment, consult your owner's manual or seek advice from the dealer who honors your equipment warranty.